LIBERIA IN NEED OF EDUCATION (LINE)

THE NEED FOR SOUND PRIMARY AND SECONDARY EDUCATION IN LIBERIA IS AN IMPERATIVE. EDUCATION ENABLES A PEOPLE TO THINK CREATIVELY AND ACT PRODUCTIVELY IN THE PROCESS OF NATION-BUILDING

Dr. Nyonbeor A. Boley, Sr.

DORRANCE
PUBLISHING CO
EST. 1920
PITTSBURGH, PENNSYLVANIA 15238

Dorrance Publishing Co
585 Alpha Drive
Pittsburgh, PA 15238
Visit our website at *www.dorrancebookstore.com*

ISBN: 979-8-8852-7101-1
eISBN: 979-8-8852-7828-7

Table of Contents

This tiny book is dedicated to all the future leaders of the Republic of Liberia, who are today's students.

May it be well with you, always.

Acknowledgments

We know from pioneering time that no author writes alone. Authors usually stand on the shoulders of those who have written and published materials long before them. In this regard, I am indebted to the publisher of *Dependence, Underdevelopment, and Persistent Conflict* on the political economy of Liberia, edited by Eckhard Hinzen and Robert Kappel, in which they discussed in detail the impact of the foreign enclaves; Rodney Carlisle's *Sovereignty for Sale* provides an excellent description and history of the development of Liberia's "flag of convenience" in which Maritime exploited the already greedy elite of Liberia ruling class; *Growth Without Development: An Economic Survey of Liberia*, edited by Robert W. Clower and others; *Country Economic Memorandum*, prepared by the Ministry of Planning and Economic Affairs for a donor meeting in 1983, which takes up at length the economic situation in Liberia in 1983, its causes, and the new PRC government effort to stabilize the economy and Liberia—a country study, edited by Harold D. Nelson.

Having read through most of these published materials, it became my considered conclusion that Liberia as a nation needs sound education and well-informed citizenry who can put Liberia on the stage of academic and economic competitiveness in West Africa and around the world. Liberia needs citizens with natural skills, foresightedness, frugality, and commitment to patriotism or love of country to lead Liberia to improvement and higher heights.

Introduction

At various times in the history of humankind, nations and peoples have recovered from economic destitution in remarkably short period of time. For example, the physical devastation of Japanese and German industrial cities during World War II did not prevent these nations from rising from the rubble to become major industrial economic powers in the postwar world. Numerous confiscations of the wealth of Jews in Europe or of the Chinese in Southeast Asia have been followed by their rising again to prosperity and wealth. In the United States, penniless refugees from Cuba, Korea, Vietnam, and Hmong have begun in their most menial occupations but, within one generation, produced a business-owning middle class in the very same United States of America. The Nigerian-Biafran bloody civil war, which nearly wiped out two-thirds of the Igbo nation, did not prevent the Igbos from becoming both the academic and business power house of modern day Nigeria. Also, the bloody history of the Hutu and Tutsi conflict which stained the twentieth century, in which more than 920,000 died, did not prevent Rwanda from rising from the rubble to become one of the most desirable African countries to invest in. Liberia experienced a 14-year civil war nearly 25 years ago. Liberia has not recovered from it.

The key to all of these phenomena or situations is that the destruction of physical capital or financial capital—though very painful—does not touch a nation's or people's human capital, which is the deciding factor in all of these situations. Conversely, the transfer of vast amounts of physical capital or financial assets has failed to create prosperity in many developing countries, including Liberia, or among many poorer classes, races, and ethnic groups within a given welfare system. In those cases as well, it is the human capital that is economically decisive and the visible investment of secondary importance. Visible physical capital, such as factories, power dams, oil refineries, is always in the process of deterioration, whether at a slower or a faster rate. Financial assets likewise are constantly being consumed in order to live in our world. Wealth in both forms will have to be replaced, even in the normal course of events. What war does is to speed up this process of wealth exhaustion and its need for replenishment. Accordingly, the real source of wealth in both normal and abnormal situations is the ability to produce human capital, not the inventory of goods, equipment, or paper assets in existence at a given time.

Human capital takes many forms, of which formal education or schooling is the most visible, but not for that reason any more important than natural skills, discipline, organizational talents, foresight, frugality, or love of country. Human capital is not all a human achievement, nor simply to the merits of those who having to possess it. What is economically salient is that differences in human capital produce large differences in results, reflected in vast gaps in standards of living, both domestically and internationally. Politically, these vast differences promote envy, resentment, and suspicious of exploitation among the less fortunate, and more arrogance or guilt among the more fortunate.

What we need in Liberia is the development of human capital with sound education, self-discipline, foresight, frugality, organizational skills, and a commitment to country. Before discussing why these fine qualities may be lacking in Liberia today, I shall discuss a brief history of Liberia education system to include the "Motto of Liberia" as an obstacle to integration in Liberia as well as to development of natural skills, organizational skills, foresight, frugality, and a commitment to country.

A Brief History of Liberia Education System and What Went Wrong

When all West African nations gained independence from their colonial masters, Liberia was more than 100 years old as an independent nation. For example, Liberia was 110 years old as an independent nation when the Republic of Ghana gained independence in 1957 from the British. Liberia was 101 years old when Guinea and Senegal gained independence in 1958, 103 years old when Nigeria and Cameroon gained independence in 1960, and 104 years old as an independent republic when Sierra Leone gained independence in 1961. But to date and at the time of this publication, Liberia is the least developed nation in West Africa in all categories, including quality of education, agriculture, economics, sense of frugality, foresight, natural skills, patriotism, and the national commitment of nation-building.

As a born Liberian, it pains my heart to have to write this tiny book and in this manner, but the truth is so because it is so. Further, we know from research and history that the best way to be honest is to confront the truth. The fact of the matter is that Liberia was run by bad governments and uninformed and uneducated individuals in most of its history, except with a few presidents that included Presidents

Tubman, Tolbert, and Samuel Doe. The historical facts are there to validate the claims of this author. What we as Liberians can do now is to look ahead and rebuild our nation after the invasion of Liberia led by some Liberians that resulted to a 14 years of an unnecessary civil war. We have to now develop a spirit of commitment to patriotism, frugality, foresightedness, and organizational skills building. With this commitment, we can develop the right human capital needed to rebuild Liberia's education system. I am confident that present-day Liberians will see the mistakes of the past and chart a new course for a better and greater Liberia. At least, this is my hope.

The founding fathers who settled down in present-day Liberia in the nineteenth century were not educated compared to other founding fathers of West African countries. For example, the first president of Liberia, Honorable Joseph Jenkins Roberts, who later became the first president of Liberia College, did not complete elementary school. It should be underscored that, with the exception of Liberia, all first presidents of West African countries earned at least a minimum of secondary education before becoming heads of state. For example, the first president of Nigeria, Dr. Nnamdi Bejamin Azikiwe, had a Ph.D; so did the first president of Ghana, Dr. Kwame Nkruman. The presidents of Sierra Leone, Honorable Siaka Stevens and Cameroon's Honorable Ahmadou Babatoura Ahidjo, both completed secondary schools. The Republic of Guinea's first president, Honorable Ahmed Sekou Toure completed secondary school and attended the French Technical College but was expelled for making trouble. These neighboring countries' presidents started their leadership with strong foresight to educate their entire countries. That said, the first individual to earn a bachelor's degree before becoming president of Liberia was the honorable William Richard Tolbert, Jr, nineteenth president of

Liberia. Although he did not complete secondary school, Liberia's eighteenth president, the honorable William V. S. Tubman, was the only president in my judgment with real foresight, organizational skills, natural skills, and patriotism to have led Liberia as president. All other presidents before him did not have such qualities.

It should also be noted that "American educational activity abroad or outside the US began with the founding of Liberia as a settlement of the American Colonization Society (ACS) for freed slaves. Although the society was non-denominational, it was supported and largely dominated by churchmen. Prominent among these churchmen were James Monroe (for whom Monrovia is named), Andrew Jackson, Henry Clay, Daniel Webster, and Bushrod Washington. These men subscribed to the evangelistic sentiments. Liberia was therefore seen not only as a home for freedmen but also as a center for the Christianization of the African Continent" (T. W. Livingston, p. 246). That said, the overarching objective for the establishment of education in Liberia during the formative years was because the "Republic of Liberia ought to have within itself the means of educating all of its citizens for all the duties of public and private life." It was certainly against this background that Professor Simon Greenleaf, the Harvard University Dean of the Law School who single-handily copied the US Constitution to serve as the Constitution of Liberia, led the effort to establish Liberia College in 1862. The college was started with two professors—Rev. Alexander Crowmwell and Professor Dr. Edward Wilmot Blyden, who opened the door of the college with seven students (https://ul.edu.lr/about/history).

From the very beginning in Liberia, public primary and secondary schools for the Americo-Liberians' children were established very early as church-sponsored schools for the citizenry of Liberia. Generally, these schools were expected to provide primary and secondary education that would permit their children to ultimately work in offices or to study for professions such as law and theology. In the nineteenth century and first half of the twentieth century, no attention was given to education of Liberia's indigenous population. Early attempts to educate children from the hinterland was resisted. Further, an earlier Americo-Liberian government was not financially equipped to consider educating the entire country and their control over the indigenous population on the coast, let alone the hinterland.

There were a few mission schools in the nineteenth century and several more in the first third of the twentieth century, but all were wards of Americo-Liberian families.

In 1912, a centralized educational system under a cabinet-level official was established as the Department of Education. It encompassed only the five coastal counties of Cape Mount, Montserrado, Bassa, Sinoe, and Maryland—and chiefly served the Americo-Liberians living there. Beyond the establishment in 1929 of the Booker T. Washington Institute (BWI) and a teacher training college by a combination of American philanthropic and religious interests, very little else of significance of education occurred in Liberia until end of World War II and Tubman's inauguration. Before the war, private and mission schools accounted for more than three-fourths of the educational facilities in the country. For the most part, formal instruction at mission schools was limited to primary level. In the pre-World War II period and later, children of the Americo-Liberia elite were sent to neighboring African territories or to Europe or the United States for secondary education, partly because of the prestige of doing so and partly because Liberian schools were not highly regarded in neighboring territories. There were exceptions, one of which was the College of West Africa, a Methodist secondary school long established in Monrovia with advanced-level instructors from the West Indies.

In the post-World War II era, economic growth and an awareness of social developments elsewhere in other African countries stimulated the government of Liberia involvement in the education of indigenous Liberians and with it the reorganization of the school system in 1961. That reorganization under President Tubman, which included mission and private schools, established a structure that persisted into the 1980s. At the base was preprimary (A, B, C, Primer I, and Primer II) education for children aged four and five; elementary schooling for children aged six to 12; junior and senior high schools for 13 years and older—each level having a three-year curriculum; and postsecondary education.

In the early 1980s, there were still significant differences in school attendance between certain coastal counties and the rural ones. Despite the growth in Liberia's total enrollment, only a little more than one-half the six to 12-year age cohort was in primary school in 1980, a proportion much smaller than that common in other West African countries. Moreover, only one-fourth of those started in kindergarten completed the sixth grade; still fewer went to junior high or middle school. Between 15 and 20 percent of the 12- to 20-year of age cohort were in secondary or high school. Only about half of those who finished junior high completed senior high school, as has been the case ("Liberia – A Country Study," p. 32).

The drop-out rate at the primary level has reflected the teachers' inadequate training in both substance and teaching skills—especially those teachers in the rural areas—and the unavailability of materials, including textbooks. All textbooks in Liberia were written by American writers or English writers. Furthermore, the use of English as the language of instruction from the beginning of the republic has been a major hurdle for most Liberian students whose mother tongue was a local African language and who were the first members of their families to attend school. Those who enrolled in secondary schools have managed to surmount these difficulties. That said, the quality of their education has been so poor that remedial work, especially in mathematics and science, has frequently been necessary.

A further serious obstacle to attendance at secondary schools has been their sparse distribution, especially in the rural areas, and the lack of dormitory accommodations for those who must come from afar. Local arrangements have, for the most part, not been available, or have been too costly or expensive, or students who lived with America-Liberian families have been required to perform so many chores for their household in which they lived that school attendance and studies at home were hindered.

Very smaller ratios of girls to boys occurred in the upper levels of primary school and continued throughout junior and senior high schools in both rural and urban areas. Although changes have been taking place, indigenous Liberians have been less than enthusiastic about sending girls to school. Moreover, Liberian children did not start school at the age of six, as educational authorities preferred, but later. Girls may therefore be at the marrying or childbearing age by the time they reach the fourth or fifth grade, and they leave school.

All young kids through the ninth grade (junior high school) have, in principle, the same educational experience. Preprimary (Primer I and Primer II, or A, B, C as they are called locally) have, in principle, the same educational experience. These preprimary schools are intended to introduce children aged five to six to have a school environment but have also been opened to older children who do not have English as a mother tongue in order to introduce them to the language before they enter primary school. The curriculum in primary and junior high schools has been a general one; all students take the same courses from textbooks written in the United States and brought to

Liberia by the government. A little more than half of school time has been devoted to general studies, about one-third to science and mathematics, and the remainder to "work oriented courses," primarily agriculture, carpentry, domestic science, and the like. At the junior high school level, additional attention was supposed to be paid to science and mathematics, but much of this work was at a remedial level.

In addition to a standard academic course, vocational, agricultural, and commercial instruction has been ordered in senior high schools. The oldest of the vocational schools is the Booker Washington Institute (BWI) located in Kakata, but others have been established, and some of the mining companies, including LAMCO, Bong Mines, and Firestone offered training in mechanical and electrical work to a small numbers of students whose parents worked for these companies.

Government expenditures on education in Liberia were very low compared with those of other West African countries. Moreover, much of what was spent went to postsecondary education, leading to improvements in its quality but leaving primary and secondary students lacking materials like textbooks and adequate and trained teachers. Most of the funds for primary and secondary schools were expended on salaries for teachers, but these were so low that the best educated of them went on to other jobs as soon as they could find them instead of teaching. Much was made in the 1970s and 1980s of textbooks often imported from the United States, which contained material that have very little or no relevance for life in Liberia. The sheer lack of textbooks was a threat to real learning in Liberia. It was estimated in the late 1970s and early 1980s that 75 percent of the students had no textbooks. Also widely lacking were such simple teaching materials as blackboards, crayons, and erasers. Even scarcer were lack of laboratory facilities for secondary-school science classes. Most night schools did not have laboratory facilities even though chemistry, physics, and biology were taught in those schools.

There were plans and programs in place in the early 1980s to deal with these academic-related problems. Teacher training and the development of adequate textbooks were given particular priority. The teacher training institutes established in the 1970s were turning out far more teachers than had been the case just a decade earlier. Notwithstanding, the number being trained annually in the late 1970s and early 1980s was not enough to meet anticipated requirements for an expanding school system or to replace the many poorly and inadequately trained teachers of the 1960s. Moreover, programs for in-service teacher training had not been developed. The effects of the textbook program were not appreciated until mid-1984.

In 1984, there were three significant postsecondary institutions in Liberia:

- The University of Liberia, a government institution in Monrovia, which was founded in 1862 as Liberia College and became a full university in 1952. The university now has four campuses—Capitol Hill; Fendall; a medical school at Fendall campus; and Starz Sinji campus located in Sinji, Grand Cape Mount County;
- Cuttington University College at Suakoko, which was administered and financially supported by the Episcopal Church with help with government subsidy; and
- The William V. S. Tubman College of Technology, a government institution founded in 1978 and located in Maryland County.

The largest of these institutions was the University of Liberia, which in 1981 had more than 3,300 students (University of Liberia Archive).

Established after World War II, it incorporated Liberia College as the college of liberal arts in 1952. Other faculties included business, agriculture, forestry, science, technology, law, and medicine. Business college attracted more than one-third of all students, followed by liberal arts and science and technology. There were more graduates in liberal arts than science and technology, however.

Cuttington University College, reestablished in 1949 having been closed in 1928, had between 500 to 550 students in 1981. They were enrolled in fields of study that ranged from economics and theology to nursing. The largest number of students studied economics, while fewer studied business, education, and nursing.

In 1981, only three years old by then, the William V. S. Tubman College of Technology had fewer than 200 hundred students, most of them in their first year of study. The institution was expected to award associate degrees in engineering technology, and it offered specialization in civil, mechanical, electrical, and electronic engineering and in architecture.

Until the Tolbert Administration in the early 1970s, the University of Liberia offered little more than a secondary-school education and not a very good one at that ("Liberia – A Country Study," p. 134). Thus, West African countries considered University of Liberia graduates at that time as "form six graduates with degrees." Moreover, because it drew upon the indigenous population for most of its students, the university had a student body that did not regard a higher education as a right conferred by social status. Many Americo-Liberians went to the University of Liberia as a rite of passage, however, and graduation in a given year was often the basis for the formation of social clubs that played a significant role in political life. Most of these Americo-Liberian graduates did not bother to go to graduate schools abroad because their positions in government were secured. In contrast to the University of Liberia academic work, Cuttington University College had higher standards for admission and graduation.

Shortly after the coup, the Doe Administration apparently encouraged the university not to only grow but to also improve its standards. Much of the improvement involved the participation of indigenous Liberians who had acquired graduate degrees from abroad—often in the United States—as faculty members. By the mid-1980s, a great and substantial proportion of the student body was of tribal origin. The improvement in the quality of the faculty and the student body and the change in the social and ethnic background of many students led to sustained awareness academically and politically. All these upward improvements ended with the senseless 14-year civil war from which Liberia has not recovered.

Further, under the eyes of a transitional military regime pledged to the restoration of civilian rule, the outlines of Liberia's second republic were taking real shape in the late 1984. If hope for the new government were realized, it would be far more democratic than its predecessors, which since the mid-nineteenth century had functioned as instruments for the perpetuation of a political aristocracy drawn from Americo-Liberian settler families. The ruling elite remained indifferent to the plight of ordinary people, especially the indigenous people living in rural Liberia. Advanced education and economic development for all Liberians were never the goals of the oligarchy. When that ruling class was removed because of corruption, nepotism, incompetency, and indifference to the plight of indigenous Liberians, they paved their way back into political power through trickery—violent invasion and total nationwide destruction. All of this invasion of their own country could have been avoided if the descendants of Americo-Liberia families had any interest in the development of Liberia.

The Love of Liberty Brought Us Here - Symbol of Disintegration

As a sovereign state since the year of 1847, Liberia is the oldest independent country in Africa, and also an anomaly when compared with the other independent countries. All the other African nations shared a legacy of having once been colonized and exploited by European powers. Only Liberia had a "colonial era" in which a tiny minority—alien in origin, lifestyle, culture, and habits of thought processes—was made up solely of black people; black people ruling black people. What actually passes for the Liberian version of a colonial experience began in the early nineteenth century with the arrival of freed American slaves sent from the United States by private colonization societies to settle along the coast of West Africa. The territories the black settlers initially acquired from the indigenous Africans living there was purchased by the American Colonization societies and other religious groups.

The early settlers brought with them very few skills and social habits acquired in the United States and other countries in the Western Hemisphere, particularly a preference for the white landowners' way of life they had witnessed and experienced in the American southern

11

states during their years of dehumanizing servitude. Viewed as evidence or symbol of success, attributes such proper attire and antebellum architectural style became important elements of the culture they formed in the new West African nation. A constitution copied or modeled on that of the United States was written for the new independent country by a Harvard University Dean of Law School, Professor Simon Greenleaf as the American pattern was followed in establishing the Liberian system of government—three branches of government—an executive, judiciary, and legislative. The country's flag copied the red, blue, and white design of its United States counterpart, its administrative subdivisions were designated as counties, and in many instances, towns and counties were given American placenames. Some of these names include Greenville, Buchanan, Maryland, and many more. The name chosen for the new republic is Liberia, meaning "land of the free," and the motto inscribed on its official coat of arms proclaimed to all the people of the African Continent and the world that "The Love of Liberty Brought Us Here," not the love of country or to integrate with the indigenous people and build a functioning government and country, I may add.

Certainly, this kind of motto was only meaningful to the settlers and their descendants, who by this time called themselves Americo-Liberians. This motto has no meaning to the indigenous people who accommodated them. From the outset, this increasingly elite group discriminated against the indigenous Africans, whose presence and freedom in the region dated from the eleventh century. The settlers referred to the indigenous as "uncivilized," "inferior," "nonchristian," and "aborigines," who were content or happy to live in a tribal setting in accordance with "primitive" traditions of their ancestors. The indigenous were treated much or exactly in the same manner as were their counterparts in neighboring African territories colonized by white European powers. The America-Liberians thought they were now the new colonial powers in Liberia. Thus a gap was created between the two elements of Liberia's population from the very beginning. This gap was to become a hindrance to the emergence of a sense of patriotism, nationalism, and foresightedness and would remain a latent source of social unrest, hatred, bitterness, and ultimately, conflict. In surrounding countries, the British and French colonizers withdrew during the mid-twentieth century, leaving the African majority to manage its own future. But Liberia's minority colonizers were an integral part of the country and did not leave, even though they had no initiative, foresight, patriotism, or natural skills to build an integrated nation for all Liberians. Further, the first set of America-Liberian population had no real education as they were taken from plantations in the American south.

The America-Liberians, who really never exceeded more than 5 percent of the population of Liberia, settled in the urban centers or areas they formed along the Atlantic Ocean coast and developed a society based on cultural models they have imported from the United States. They showed no interest in learning the language(s) of indigenous Liberians, the majority element of the population. For over 100 years, the settlers had nothing to do with the indigenous Liberian population and encouraged them to remain in their homelands in the interior of the country. Exceptions were made, however, when cheap labor was needed on the large-scale estates established by America-Liberians in the exact tradition of the planter aristocracy once common on the plantations in America south. Ironically, forcible recruitment and compulsory labor practices were often reminiscent of the slavery that was much part of the America-Liberian experience and heritage. Preoccupied with its own development goals, this select minority effectively excluded the indigenous majority from Liberia's political and economic life for 133 years. With the help of US gun boat, the Americo-Liberian minority imposed annual taxation on the indigenous majority. These are the effects of a motto that represented 5 percent of the country with no formula for integration.

Because of the lack of initiative, foresightedness, and natural skills, the republic led an isolated, impoverished, and often precarious existence until well into the twentieth century. The minority ruling class managed the affairs of the country through borrowed loans as they were given free food and clothing from the Unites States during the first 100 years of existence. That being said, economic development was retarded by the decline of markets for Liberian goods in the late nineteenth century and by indebtedness on a series of loan repayments.

Two very important events occurred in leasing Liberia from its self-imposed isolation. The first was the grant of a large concession to US-owned Firestone Plantations Company; that move became a first step in the modernization of the Liberian economy. The second event occurred during World War II, when United States began providing technical and economic assistance that enabled Liberia to make economic progress and introduce social change. The United States built the Roberts International Airport (RIA) during this period.

In 1944, Liberia began to experience positive growth in many directions. President William Vacanarat Shadrach Tubman was inaugurated as the eighteenth president of Liberia. He introduced the Unification Policy to bring indigenous or tribal Africans into the mainstream of Liberian political life for the first time by establishing four new political subdivisions. The Open Door Policy, which he announced in his inaugural address that year, invited large-scale foreign investment that further aided in transforming the Liberian economy. President Tubman was foresighted and imbued with natural skills in the spirit of nation-building. During his long administration, Liberia education system advanced with the establishment of the Monrovia Consolidated School Systems (MCSS), the establishment of the A. M. Dogliotti College of Medicine at the University of Liberia in 1968, and the John F. Kennedy Memorial Hospital as both the largest hospital in the country and also as a teaching hospital for the newly established medical school that same year.

Wide disparities in the distribution of income and public services were continuing sources of unrest during the new administration after the death of President Tubman. Despite the strides made during Tubman's administration that of his successor, President William Richard Tolbert was unable to satisfy the rising economic expectations and demands for greater participation in political decision-making by the indigenous majority. Opposition to the America-Liberian elite mounted, and dissatisfaction was expressed at every level over the rampant corruption and nepotism associated with the Tolbert administration.

A time comes in the history of a people when they get tired of been exploited and disrespected; a time comes when the people can no longer remain guests in their own fatherland. That time came on April 12, 1980, when a successful military coup was staged by a group of non-commissioned junior officers all of tribal origins led by Master Sergeant Samuel Kanyon Doe, and President Tolbert was assassinated. Constituting themselves as the People's Redemption Council (PRC), Doe and his associates seized total control of the government and brought an end to Liberia "first republic" after 133 years of oligarchy.

Educational activities during the early years of President Doe's administration witnessed some improvements. More and more native-born Liberians who have completed graduate schools abroad joined the faculty at the University of Liberia. The Fendall Campus was renovated as buses provided free-of-charge transportation for students to and from Monrovia. The new administration came as a beacon light of hope for all Liberians who yearn for advanced education and real freedom. A new graduate school was added to the undergraduate programs at the University of Liberia. In fact, professors and other well-learned academicians were contracted from Nigeria and other African countries to advance and accelerate Liberia education system.

That all came to a halt when nearsighted Liberians invaded their own country for absolutely no good reason. During the civil war years, the educational infrastructure was particularly attacked, along with government ministries. The only thing that descendants of Americo-Liberians needed to do to return to political power was to recruit very few members of the Gio tribe from Nimba County to destabilize the nation. They were very successful with an invasion of Liberia that led to the destruction of the education system as well as anything that represented progress during the Doe's presidency.

The World Come to the Rescue

The Ebola crisis was both a curse and a blessing in Liberia. It was a curse because so many innocent Liberians died during the Ebola pandemic; and a blessing because as a direct result of the Ebola crisis, the world came to the aid of Liberia. For the first time, the world saw how poor Liberia's infrastructure, including health care system and education system were. The first aid organizations came as the PREVAIL, PEER, and then the LCPS.

The Partnership for Research on Ebola Vaccine in Liberia (PREVAIL), a Liberia-US clinical trial partnership established to develop a vaccine for Ebola survivors, was first launched to save lives in Liberia. PREVAIL was very closely followed by PEER.

The Partnership for Enhanced Engagement Research Liberia (PEER) was sponsored by the US Agency for International Development (USAID) and implemented by the United States National Academies of Sciences, Engineering, and Medicine. In the aftermath of the Ebola outbreak of 2014-2015, hundreds of Ebola survivors had developed a range of many diseases, including ocular conditions from persistent Ebola infections. PEER stepped in to prevent the spread of Ebola-related diseases.

Liberian College of Physicians and Surgeons (LCPS) was launched as a medical school to upgrade medical training at the A. M. Dogliotti College of Medicine (AMD), University of Liberia. LCPS is currently providing technical assistance towards medical curriculum reform and overall research capacity at the AMD. LCPS is the sole post-graduate residency training program in Liberia and is an independent institution from the University of Liberia. Founded by the Liberia-US partnership in 2013 in response to shortage of trained physicians in Liberia, LCPS provides training in the clinical disciplines of internal medicine, obstetrics and gynecology, pediatrics, and surgery. In other words, the LCPS is helping to upgrade Liberia medical education to meet its accreditation in WAHO.

In 2017, a USAID publication stated that:

A. M. Dogliotti College of Medicine (AMD) is at the national level accredited by the National Council of Higher Education of Liberia and is an accredited program under the University of Liberia. AMD is also included in the WHO World Directory of Medical Schools. Regionally, or in West Africa, medical colleges are accredited by the West African Health Organization (WAHO) following ECOWAS guidelines for all medical schools in the region. Currently, AMD is not accredited by WAHO.

Therefore, there was an urgent need for the LCPS to step in to assist Liberia in reforming the country's medical school curriculum in preparation for regional accreditation.

In addition to the PREVAIL, PEER, and LCPS Operations in Liberia, USAID sponsored organizations were brought in Liberia for the development of Liberia education system. These organizations included the Global Partnership for Education (GPE) and Learning Squared Liberia (LSL). The GPE and LSL came to the rescue after the 14 years of a senseless civil war to rebuild Liberia's education system from the primary school level in coordination with Liberia Ministry of Education(MOE).

According to the Global Partnership for Education in Liberia (GPE):

> *...the education sector in Liberia faces a complex set of challenges related to rebuilding and recovery from the civil war, constrained national finances, poor infrastructure and the Ebola epidemic. These challenges include poor learning outcomes, overage enrollment, huge number of out-of-school children, wasted government resources because of 'ghost' teachers and unskilled teachers, and many unqualified teachers in the entire country.*

On a systemic level, there are no national school quality standards and capacity and resourcing at county and district levels which require improvement. The education sector also faces very serious equity challenges including important geographic differences in access to quality education in Liberia.

In order to address these challenges, GPE-Liberia has developed a strategic response in its "Getting to Best Education Sector Plan" for 2017 to 2022. The plan consists of nine programs:

1. Establishing effective school quality improvement and accountability systems;
2. Improving the efficiency and performance of education management system;

3. Improving access to high quality early childhood education for all children;

4. Providing quality alternative and accelerated education pathways for average and out-of-school children and young people;

5. Improving the efficiency, effectiveness, and satisfaction of the teaching workforce of Liberia;

6. Ensuring that teachers have access to high quality instructional materials and assessment tasks;

7. Mainstreaming gender and school health across the education sector;

8. Improving the quality and relevance of technical and vocational education and training; and

9. Leveraging regional and international partnerships and expertise, targeting market demand for critical skills and increasing the efficiency of education expenditure.

(References:
https://www.globalpartnership.org/where-we-work/Liberia)

Learning Squared Liberia (LSL) has its overarching objective of improving education for the children of Liberia and developing the capacity of individuals and communities to build a healthy and thriving democracy in Liberia.

LSL observed that "access to education in Liberia is a considerable challenge, especially in rural and underserved communities around the country." According to UNICEF, Liberia has the world's largest out-of-school children. Learning Squared Liberia (LSL) currently works with community, women, and rural schools to provide practical solutions that improve access to quality education and foster an economic and social development for rural women.

To clearly accomplish their goals and objectives, LSL provides community-based solutions that support Liberian women to generate income to contribute to their children's education and help them work their way through poverty and improve the quality of life for themselves and their families. Also, LSL offers many opportunities for Liberian women to generate income through a program set up as a "Social Microfinance" revolving loan for women to thrive. To this end, LSL developed a 3E model of multiplying the power of education in Liberia, especially in rural and underserved communities:

- **Engage:** Identify the needs and challenges faced by children for obtaining education and together find a solution.
- **Educate:** Creating access to quality and affordable education and opportunities for children in Liberia.
- **Empower:** Help women create a sustainable income to help fund their children's education and pay for basic household needs.

According to UNICEF/LSL, in Liberia:

- 15-20 percent of children ages 6-15 do not go to school;
- 46 percent of children do not complete primary school;
- 36 percent of primary school teachers are unqualified; and
- 30 percent of secondary school teachers are unqualified.

This sickening statistics is a direct result of the unnecessary 14-year civil war brought upon the country by descendants of Americo-Liberian families.

UNICEF/Liberia observation: "Liberia education system is emerging from a prolonged and brutally destructive period of civil conflict or unrest." Longstanding impact from the civil war compounded by the 2014-2015 school closure due to Ebola Viral Disease (EVD) outbreak continues to take a toll on the very weak and fragile education system in Liberia. Liberia is significantly behind in all African countries in nearly all education statistics. For example, the "primary school net enrollment rate"—the percentage of primary age students attending primary grades—is 44 percent for Liberia. This is lowest category in West Africa.

After 14 years of civil war, which resulted in the total destruction of much of the country's workforce, Liberia is still in the process of rebuilding its education system. USAID, in concert with other donors, works with the Liberia Ministry of Education (MOE) to address the education challenges related to access, quality of instruction, and improved governance of the education system.

USAID's education programs focus on improving the quality of teaching and learning (especially in early grade reading) and increasing equitable access to safe learning opportunities for girls and for youth who missed out on education due to postwar reconstruction and a very weak education system. USAID is also helping to improve the quality of curricula, teaching and management staff instructional and learning resources, data systems, and policy environment essential to providing basic education services to all Liberians. USAID programming also taps into the energy and dynamism of Liberia's large youth population through a new activity that emphasizes developing the capacity of young Liberians to be key players in their country's journey to self-reliance. Up to the time of this book, USAID developed all kinds of programs to help Liberia improve its standing in the educational arena of West Africa and of the world. For example, USAID has developed programs such as the "Accelerated Learning for Overage and Out-Of-School Children," "Early Grade Reading Support," and "Preparing the Next Generation of Liberian Civil Service Leaders." This is all good news for Liberia.

Under the impressive topic, "Preparing the next generation of Liberian civil service leaders," USAID is implementing the President's Young Professionals Program (PYPP) to help the next generation of Liberia's civil service leaders. PYPP supports a cohort (Class IX) of young 20 Liberian college graduates who have been placed in government ministries, national agencies, and private sector institutions on a two-year fellowship. The activity balances the government's immediate need for competent junior staff with the longer-term goals of increasing the capacity of the civil service and at the same time preparing a new generation of talented youth for leadership roles in government. PYPP recruits, places, trains, and mentors the participants, and is also piloting greater private sector engagement by placing some of its Class IX fellows in private sector organizations. With both public and private placements, this activity is developing a new generation of professionals who will enhance private sector investment, increase quality service delivery, and instill sustainable good governance practices in institutions where they are assigned. This USAID created PYPP will constitute what I refer to as the development of human capital for Liberia. In any development effort, it is the human capital that is economically and academically decisive, where visible investment stands at a secondary level. Now is the time to develop Liberia's human capital. USAID has begun such creative effort. Young Liberians must seize this opportunity to re-build the country.

No amount of external support or foreign aid will improve Liberia education system unless Liberians truly develop and maintain a sense of commitment to education, improving of natural skills, foresightedness, frugality, and patriotism.

As indicated earlier in this text, the development of human capital takes many forms of which formal sound education stands at the top of the list. Liberians need sound education, improvement in natural skills building, frugality, foresightedness, and a commitment to patriotism. With such commitment, Liberia as a country will develop and maintain the necessary human capital it needs for progress. The USAID PYPP Program is a necessary first step.

The Role of Sound Formal Education
Sound formal education is as important as the air we breathe to stay alive. It is the most important possession a person can have that can't be taken away. Sound education is beneficial in many ways, and many aspects of our life, especially in the spirit of nation building. Education helps to open the door of opportunities. As Louis Pasteur reminded us, "Chance favors the prepared mind." Education opens a whole world of opportunities for anyone who seeks it. Education gives us knowledge, which is power. With sound education, nobody can fool you and lure you into recruitment to commit violence against innocent people. A sound and educated person is less likely to be influenced to do something which is not legally or morally right. An uneducated individual who lives in abject poverty often turn to illegal ways such as theft and robbery to solve his/her problems. An uneducated youth can easily be recruited to fight war he had no plan to participate in.

Sound and formal education is needed for the economic growth of a nation. For example, China, Japan, Australia, Great Britain, the USA, and other developed countries with high literacy rates are leaders in the world today because they have an educated workforce with useful skills. Education is, indeed, vital for the economic growth and prosperity of a nation. Finally, being culturally and socially educated help people connect with other people around the world. Sound education minimizes ignorance, hatred, and bitterness among people of our one world.

Natural Skills Improvement

Natural skills improvement is also another aspect of the human condition second to sound academic education. Natural skills development is a vital tool that empowers people who may not have academic degrees to have a reasonable standard of living, it is a vital tool to safeguard the future and overall satisfaction for an individual. It is an important aspect of life that enhances employability in today's globalized economy. Natural skills are as important as one's academic status. An individual who possesses both natural skills and sound academic status is an asset to nation-building in the true sense of the word.

Natural skills development means more and better job opportunities; it is key to the growth of the economy, expanding businesses and job creation. Natural skills include problem-solving skills, self-confidence in the things one does, interpersonal skills, excellent communication, adaptability to situation, and personal integrity. Natural skills building can improve the life of workers, their prospect for a better tomorrow, and self-reliance.

Frugality

Frugality, by definition, is the quality of being frugal, sparing, prudent in the consumption of consumable goods or resources such as food, time, how money is spent, and avoiding waste and lavishness or extravagance. Frugal can also be defined as careful management of material resources, being thrifty. A frugal government does not waste money on very expensive or luxury cars for government workers. A frugal government spends money and other resources in a very prudent manner. Frugality needs to be put in practice in Liberia. Certainly, frugality and foresight go hand-in-hand.

Foresight

Foresight is the ability to plan for what will happen in the future. For example, foresight is predicting what will happen in the stock market before it actually happens. Another example for having foresight is knowing to save money into an emergency fund in case of natural or man-made disaster. Foresight is the ability to judge correctly and clearly what is going to happen in the future and to plan your actions based on this knowledge acquired. Foresight is very critical in all areas of our lives, including major life decisions and the running of a business or government. A foresighted leader gives his country or business increased power to shape its future, even in the most turbulent times. President William V. S. Tubman had natural skills and was clearly foresighted. Liberians need to be frugal, foresighted, naturally talented to rebuild nation. Natural skills or talent is the key ingredient to a successful nation or organization.

Patriotism

Patriotism, by definition, is a devoted love, support, and defense of one's own fatherland or country. Patriotism means natural loyalty to one's country. Government employees or ordinary citizens who volunteer their time in the interest of their country are patriots. Patrote, a Greek word for patriotism, means "fellow-countryman" or lineage member of a country. Patriots are people devoted to a particular place or country in a particular way of life, which an individual believes to be the best in the world and is prepared to give his or her life to defend it. Patriotism is of its natural color defensive, both militarily and culturally. To be patriotic is to be an active citizen for the common good of one's country, to actively demonstrate love for your country by being part of the political process. Patriots don't steal from their government. True patriots do not invade their country.

The absence of patriotism is the presence of disloyalty, wasteful spending of government resources, wickedness towards your fellow citizens, and conspiracy against your government. The single substance that is lacking in most Liberians today is the spirit of patriotism. Liberians need to show more love for their country. Almost all Liberians I spoke with during the preparation of text want to leave the country for the United States of America or some European countries. Without patriotism for one's own country, it is impossible to be frugal or foresighted in manner of governance. Liberians at home and abroad need to develop and maintain a spirit of patriotism, foresightedness, frugality, and natural skills improvement as we move into the twenty-first century. This must be our collective responsibility. We can do it. So let's get to work for Liberia.

Conclusion
The Road Forward

As indicated earlier in the preface, at various times in our history, nations and peoples have recovered from economic destitution during wars. For example, the physical devastation of German and Japanese industrial cities during World War II did not prevent either nation from rising from the rubble to become major industrial economic powers in the post-war world. Even non-English speaking and penniless refugees from Cuba, South Korea, Vietnam, and Hmong who began in their most menial occupations including domestic housekeeping or picking fruits on US farms have been able to produce a business-owning middle class just within one generation of their stay in the United States of America.

These rapid developments did not happen in European countries alone. The Nigerian-Biafran bloody civil war, which nearly wept out the Igbo tribe, did not prevent the Igbos from becoming both the academic and business-owning class in present day Nigeria. Also, the bloody history of the Hutu and Tutsi conflict, which took the lives of more than 920,000, did not prevent Rwanda from rising from the chaos to become one of the best countries in Africa for investment.

Liberia experienced a 14-year civil war nearly 25 years ago. Liberia has not recovered from it.

The key to all these phenomena is that the destruction of physical capital or financial capital—though very painful—does not touch the human capital of these countries, which is the deciding factor in all these situations. Conversely, borrowing loans or the transfer of vast amounts of financial assets or money has failed to create prosperity in many developing countries, especially Liberia. Even the welfare system in the US has failed to improve the lives of many minority members of society. In those cases as well, it is the human capital that is economically decisive, and all the visible investment of secondary importance.

Human capital takes many forms, of which formal education or schooling is the most visible, but not for that reason any more important than natural skills, self-disciple, foresight, frugality, and love of country. Without love of country or patriotism, it is near impossible for the people to develop and maintain a sense of frugality and foresight, for a country whose national motto states the "love of liberty brought us here" and who has been dependent on the US from its very inception cannot develop natural skills that could lead to the building of an integrated functioning society. With a very poor educational background, Liberians need to work harder to gain the respect of the West African education system. PREVAIL, PEER, LCPS—all USAID sponsored programs—are helping to improve academic as well as economic conditions in Liberia, but the time has come for Liberians to step up and take the lead. We can do it! Let's get to work to re-build the country. When evil men plot and destroy, good men must plan and build.

Liberia academic class must begin to write textbooks for Liberian schools in their respective disciples as a necessary first step in advancing education in the country. The country cannot continue to purchase textbooks from the United States for Liberian students. This is the challenge for us all. My second publication, *Functional Anatomy and Physiology for the Busy Paramedics and EMTS* (April, 2020), is my first contribution in this effort.

Dr. Nyonbeor A. Boley, Sr.

Presidents of the Republic of Liberia

President	Term in Office	Birthplace	Comments
Joseph J. Roberts	1848-1856	Virginia (USA)	Served five two-year
Steven A. Benson	1856-1864	Maryland (USA)	Served four terms
Daniel B. Warner	1864-1868	Kentucky (USA)	Served two terms
James S. Payne	1868-1870	Virginia (USA)	Served first term
Edward J. Roye*	1870-1871	Ohio (USA)	Deposed/killed
James S. Smith	1871-1872	South Carolina (USA)	Completed Roye's term
Joseph J. Roberts	1872-1876	Virginia (USA)	Served one term
James S. Payne	1876-1878	Virginia (USA)	Served second term
Anthony W. Gardner	1878-1883	Maryland (USA)	Served three terms
Alfred F. Russel	1883-1884	Kentucky (USA)	Completed Gardner's term
Hilary R.W. Johnson	1884-1892	Liberia	Served four terms
Joseph J. Cheeseman	1892-1896	South Carolina (USA)	Elected to 3rd term, died in office.
William D. Coleman	1896-1900	Kentucky (USA)	Completed Cheeseman's term
Garretson W. Gibson	1900-1904	Maryland (USA)	Completed Coleman's term
Arthur Barclay	1904-1912	Barbados	Served two terms
Daniel E. Howard	1912-1920	Liberia	Served two terms
Charles D.B. King	1920-1930	Sierra Leone	Served three terms
Edwin J. Barclay	1930-1944	Liberia	Completed King's term, served 8 years
William V. S. Tubman*	1944-1971	Liberia	Served longest terms, died in office
William R. Tolbert	1971-1980	Liberia	Assassinated in 1980
Samuel K. Doe*	1980-1990	Liberia	Assassinated in 1990
Charles Taylor	1997-1998	Liberia	Chased out of Liberia
Ellen J. Sirleaf	2008-2016	Liberia	Served two terms
George M. Weah*	2017-present	Liberia	Serving first term.

To date, there have been only four dark-skinned presidents of Liberia. Most of the other presidents of Liberia were mullatos (children of white slave owners) and/or light-skinned individuals.

With the exception of Edward J. Roye, the first 10 presidents of Liberia (born in the USA) had no formal education. With these kinds of leaders what became of Liberia later on was bound to happen.

Interesting Pictures
of Young People and Others

This is the picture of President Joseph J. Roberts, born in Virginia, USA and became both the first president of Liberia as well as first president of Liberia College.

Students with USAID provided school supplies
With smiling faces, these young Liberians remain the hope for a better tomorrow in Liberia. Will they seize the opportunities provided by USAID in Liberia? This is my hope.

Learning Squared Liberia is dedicated to improving education and developing the capacity of individuals and communities thriving democracy.

LIBERIA

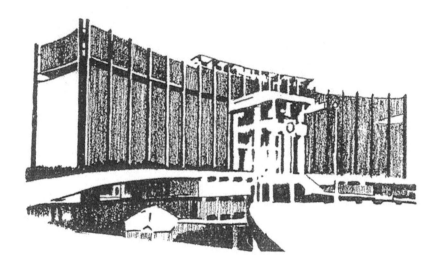
The Executive Mansion is the home of the president of Liberia.

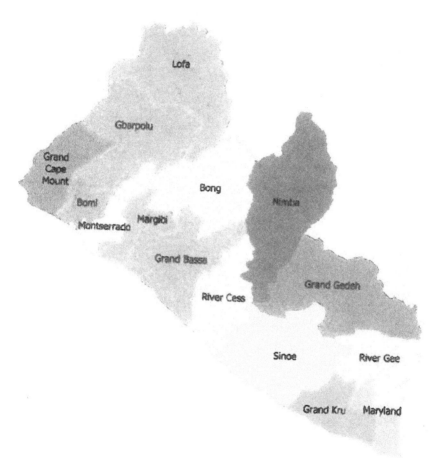